British Library Cataloguing in Publication Data

Plan your Explosive Business Growth—as simple as 2-1-4-3

Aidan J. Connolly & Kate Phillips Connolly
ISBN 9781899043798
© Aidan J. Connolly
2143plan.com

For more information on content / references please contact the author.

CONTEXT

Context Publications
Context Products Ltd
53 Mill Street
Packington
Ashby de la Zouch
Leicestershire
LE65 1WN
England

Tel: +44 (0) 1530 411337
Email: info@contextpublications.co.uk

D1265000

What people are saying about 2-1-4-3

"Looking at 'what happened' vs. spending valuable time and energy on 'where we're going'. Aidan Connolly's 2-1-4-3 approach refocuses strategic efforts to be more forward looking, forward thinking, and provocative. With a clear approach and easy tools to get started, this book is a 'how-to' that leaders need to establish a stronger vision for the future and a clear roadmap for success."

Lisa Bodell, CEO/futurethink, Author of Why Simple Wins

"Those in the global food, fiber, energy, and pharmaceutical system are part of an interrelated, interdependent structure that is constantly changing along with the adjusting mechanisms that hold the system together. One change in one part of the system affects the whole system and the institutions that help it adjust to change. These interrelationships call for collaboration and coordination over generations of owners and executives."

Ray Goldberg, George M. Moffett, Professor of Agriculture and Business, Emeritus and author of Food Citizenship: Food System Advocates in an Era of Distrust

"They say that if you "keep doin' what you're doing you'll keep gettin' what you're getting." The **2-1-4-3** approach sparks you into thinking much more creatively on how to achieve better results than you'd have previously considered possible."

Deiric McCann, Head of International Development, Genos International

"The thing about SMART - the previous gold standard for setting goals - is that it doesn't mention the how. **2-1-4-3** encourages you - insists, even - that you address this point. Even better, it asks you to look back and take into account how you've arrived at your current situation.

Often the problem with senior leadership is that they dish out goals to their teams willy-nilly - with no apparent context - and then wonder why their staff fails to achieve them. With **2-1-4-3**, the manager must think carefully before passing on goals and then can do so whilst explaining the bigger picture - leading to a far higher chance of success.

"But why?!" is often the lament of staff on the receiving end of goals from above. "What's the point?!" **2-1-4-3** takes them through the whole thought process and provides the bigger picture, not just an apparently random short-term goal. The chances of success have just risen manifold... Setting goals is easy. Achieve 20% growth! Double turnover within five years! Gain 10 new $1m customers within 12 months! Inestimably harder is working out how...

2-1-4-3 provides a perfect dialogue between all stakeholders and operators, offering a look back at what has gone on before, leading to a realistic, practical conversation about what may be possible in the future. Motivation means involvement and being part of something big. **2-1-4-3** provides this."

Floyd K Ballantyne, Managing Director, FKB Training

"Practical, accessible, effective. With **2-1-4-3,** Aidan Connolly provides a useful tool for organizations of all sizes to successfully navigate complex industry dynamics and achieve sustainable growth in today's fast-changing world. Every business leader can benefit from adopting this proven approach."

Mary Shelman, Board Director, Advisor & Speaker,
Former Director of Harvard Business School's Agribusiness Program

"China's dynamic & highly competitive business environment requires management innovation; **2-1-4-3** offers a practical framework for doing this."

Fu Wenge, Professor & Director of EMBA program at China Agricultural University

"Focusing on the end goal, and working back from there, means that you will always have sight of what you are aiming to achieve. This is so important, not only to achieve these goals but also so that you remain motivated in the process of getting there."

David Markey, Publisher, IFP Media

"You have classically, simplified complexity."

Paul A. Slattery, Leadership Development, Communications Mentor,
Development Coach to Organizations

"When constructing our three-year plan, the **2-1-4-3** model was front of our minds; we tried to use as much disruptive thinking as possible."

David O'Connor, Group General Manager, Louis Copeland & Sons

"At GE we moved from pursuing a 'make and sell' approach to a 'what to make for our markets' approach. Aidan's 2-1-4-3 model allows you to foster that culture of innovation you need to create new products, services or new customers."

Beth Comstock, former CMO of GE & author of Imagine It Forward: Courage, Creativity,
and the Power of Change

"The strength of Aidan Connolly's incisive foresight is astutely crafted in the use of the **2-1-4-3** tool as a scaffold, to induce individuals and leaders to frame the correct questions. Transformative changes in business needs a compass. Mr Connolly's guide to using the **2-1-4-3** approach may be that crucial compass, in our elusive quest for the correct questions. The pursuit of relevant answers may enable enterprises to map the convergence for profitability via the tributaries of entrepreneurial innovation."

Shoumen Palit Austin Datta, Auto-ID Labs, Department of Mechanical Engineering,
MIT and MDPnP Lab, Massachusetts General Hospital, Harvard Medical School

"In my experience, **2-1-4-3** opened the doors for all people in an organization to plan, resolve issues or even conduct a meeting. Once understood, it provides a logical basis for everyone to work together and a simple structure that eliminates the 'block' of how to write a plan and allows people to just get on with the content. Setting up a template that suits a business using **2-1-4-3** provides a simple planning tool which, once completed, sets out actions for growth and achievement of identified goals."

David Faulkner, *Global Business Development Director, Global Nutrition International and Director, David Faulkner & Associates P/L*

"For more than 25 years Aidan Connolly has driven results from leadership and sales teams around the world with an endless variety of management tools he developed himself. The most effective of all of these is **2-1-4-3.** I have observed the logic and simplicity of **2-1-4-3** engage even the most cynical mangers and drive organization commitment to the achievement of stretch goals. **2-1-4-3** is worth the small investment required to understand and implement it. Don't miss out!"

Damien McLoughlin, *Professor of Marketing, Michael Smurfit School of Business*

"This really is a phenomenal way in which one can surely address most contemporary business situations."

Anil Pathak, *Consultant*

"A real challenge for any business is to marry what traditionally 'works well' with the disruptive innovation required to grow exponentially. In this book, Aidan has set out a clear way for any organization to positively disrupt business planning and deliver ambitious long-term results in doing so."

John Herlihy, *Vice President & Managing Director (Europe, Middle East & Asia), LinkedIn*

"In a very complicated world, this is a very simple, but powerful **2-1-4-3** process that consistently delivers great results. I've seen it transform teams and companies at every level. It cuts through all the noise and clutter enabling us to focus on and act upon the things that really matter. I strongly recommend it, because it works consistently right across organizations. It's a powerful transformational tool for leadership, management, sales and coaching."

Declan Coyle, *Director, Andec Communications and author of The Green Platform*

"I plan to use with some of the companies and executives I coach and consult for in agriculture. What I love is the 'Ready, Set, Go' rhythm in this process."

Kip Pendleton, *President & CEO, Pendleton Group, LLC*

"Very simple, involves everyone, great questions pointing our thinking in the right direction, all wrapped up in a mood of ambition. Love it."

Gary O'Sullivan, *Partner, Pathfinder*

"The challenge posed by stage 4—Where you want to go—summarizes the essence of long-range strategy. This is the purview of top management. Of course, a method like 2-1-4-3 can be used by anyone at any level, but it's critical that top leadership be directly involved in defining the company we desire to become in the future. The bigger the change required—and the more significant the competitive challenges the company might face—the more the C-suite must engage in creating a '4' that isn't just an incremental iteration of the company's current '2'."

Robert C. Wolcott, Professor of Innovation, Kellogg School of Management

"Great way of challenging those involved in strategic planning to focus more on where to go rather than where one has been!"

Steve Akins, Vice President of Sales, WATT Global Media

"A bit like turning the good old SWOT analysis into OSWT, **2-1-4-3** is written in a very practical way that can be applied to any business; a very helpful, generous and a truly collaborative piece of work."

Patrick Burge, Start-up Business Advisor and Funder

"Interesting, practical approach to business planning."

Latha M N, Business Development Manager, Inboundsys

"**2-1-4-3** has helped me in my personal crusade, to build the Farm of the Future in British Columbia. While I am well versed in making pitches to politicians, business people, educators and associations it is also clear to me that when you get very excited by a project it is easy to lose focus, especially in communication and focused on the goal. The **2-1-4-3** process has allowed me to see what I need to put my attention toward, whether creating briefing documents, presentations, speeches, etc. **2-1-4-3** really made me focus on the most important goals and how to achieve them. I highly recommend it to anyone who wants to achieve success either in business or personal life!"

Christopher Bush, President, Catalyst Agri-Innovations Society

"Planning is important, but "doing" is essential—planning needs to be transformed into "real work" to create value.

Michael Boehlje, Distinguished Professor at Purdue University

"Strategies based on history too often fail because more is expected of them than they can deliver. Furthermore, there's no such thing as a mature industry—perhaps it is your strategy that is mature!"

Frank Bradley, Michael Smurfit Graduate Business School, University College Dublin

"Moderate times call for moderate responses. Immoderate times call for immoderate responses."

Tom Peters, American author including In Search of Excellence *and* The Excellence Dividend

Why another book on business planning?

Most business books make promises such as a better way to build your company, improve profitability or get sales.

Using either gimmicks or "proven" techniques (free samples, rewards programs, tier-based platforms), these are often laden with impelling jargon (Last chance! Act now! Special offer!), with exhaustive lists, tips and tools; they offer solutions for whatever problem your company faces.

So why another book on business planning? Because **2-1-4-3** doesn't offer solutions. Instead it gives you tools that can be used at any crossroads, to identify and evaluate the possibilities and create a plan for achieving your goals. It is useful for organizations of any size, is flexible enough for any industry and allows for input from a range of roles, while laying the groundwork for buy-in at all levels.

Don't be deceived by its size; a successful **2-1-4-3** will take more collective effort than a traditional business plan. As Mark Twain famously said, "I apologize for writing a long letter to you, I didn't have time to write a short one!"

The **2-1-4-3** process taps into the imagination, the experience, and the collective knowledge of the team you involve in the process, so that the benefits of their best efforts can be brought to bear on whatever opportunities, challenges, goals or aspirations the organization has in front of it.

Aidan Connolly
Chief Innovation Officer,
Vice-president, Corporate Accounts,
Alltech

Igniting change in your organization

Why do some people succeed and some fail? Why do some businesses grow spectacularly while others stagnate? Why do some people evolve while others regress?

These questions have been my quest for over 28 years of business, and millions of miles travelled flying to over 100 countries of the world.

My conclusions? Not surprisingly a positive mindset helps immeasurably, but so, too, the ability to say and write out critical goals, to have everyone in the team know what they are and be involved in defining what they are and to use a lot of creativity in reaching those goals.

In my years with Alltech the **2-1-4-3** has enabled team after team – in businesses as diverse as food, agriculture, nutrition, beverages, equipment and services – to achieve extraordinary results. Increasingly other businesses outside of ones I have been directly involved with such as a software company, a charity, a bakery, and others have also found success.

Creating teams that achieve extraordinary results is the secret sauce to business, to life. Knowing how to do it consistently has eluded many with otherwise perfect products and brilliant business plans. **2-1-4-3** gives you the ingredients to make that sauce.

Contents

Disrupting the typical business plan

Typical business planning involves building on last year's plan that was itself based on what was done the previous year, going back to the last major change or crisis in the organization.

Tweaking resources or incremental thinking is the norm; fresh thinking is rare.

Traditionally business plans use a four-step process:

1. Managers review the previous year's objectives and results.
2. They evaluate the current circumstances.
3. They create a plan and budget for the coming year.
4. They set goals for the results which the team must implement.

Substantial weight is placed on a review of the past, with the assumption that the past is essential to understanding the current operating environment, before looking to the future. For this reason, the past heavily influences the plan (usually for the next 12 months) as well as the expected outcomes. The format is linear and chronological:

1. Yesterday
2. Today
3. Future actions
4. Future results

Visually, it might look something like this:

Typical Outline for Business Planning

This is a time-consuming approach to creating a business plan, and the result is often quickly out of date. The system works best in predictable, linear environments, and there are fewer and fewer of those. Enter "disruptive thinking," which is seen as the solution: a key to creative thinking, which in turn will lead to new opportunities, and thus to exponential growth.

Disruptive thinking has indeed led to many success stories such as Uber and Airbnb but is fraught with challenges. Creating an expectation that real, substantial, disruptive change will happen can lead to dissatisfaction and resistance if any actual changes are disappointing to individuals or teams. Further, truly disruptive change is rare and takes time to integrate.

How can the productive freshness of thought be introduced in a positive way? By involving the entire team in a process that offers freedom within limits, allowing team members to bring their own creative thinking, direction and expertise to bear, creating genuine interest and investment. When compared to the old methods, the **2-1-4-3** method clearly disrupts the process:

Where we are now

How we got here

Where we want to go

What we are going to do

2-1-4-3 Strategic Planning Framework

Disruption in business

Industries and businesses are being disrupted as never before. Did the movie industry imagine the arrival of Netflix, hotels competition from Airbnb or taxis from Uber? Even listing today's disruptors makes you wonder who or what will disrupt even them.

Challenger	Industry
Linked in	Recruiting
UBER	Taxis
TESLA	Energy Storage
NETFLIX	Movie Rental
	Music Players
airbnb	Hotels
23andMe	Healthcare
PELOTON	Home Exercise
houzz	DIY Home Remodeling
duolingo	Language Learning

Could someone rethink, reengineer or disrupt your business? What would they do to reinvent it in a way that would fundamentally change the nature of competition and make what you offer, your product or your service obsolete? **2-1-4-3** can be a tool to avoid becoming out of step with your customers, making your business obsolete.

Remembering a disruptor:
Dr Pearse Lyons (1944-2018)

It's challenging for a company to lose its founder, president and owner, but especially when he is your father. Dr Pearse Lyons founded Alltech with very little capital, just $10,000 in 1980, but by the time of his passing the company's annualized turnover exceed $2 billion dollars.

From his over 40 years of business experience and since the founding of Alltech in 1980, I saw how he combined gut feeling with an uncanny sense of the trends and direction of the market. This is a common characteristic of many entrepreneurs, but as with so many entrepreneurs he did it in his own way.

Dad was never a fan of formalized, lengthy business plans and so Alltech managers long sought a solution to making planning simple and relevant. The **2-1-4-3** model has been the answer for us and our bias for action over analysis.

While his Ph.D. gave him insights into technologies and vision of how to design solutions that have become the byword in natural health in animal nutrition, part of his genius was selecting the right managers to implement his vision. Those managers representing the 131 countries in which Alltech conducts business have delivered on that vision. Communicating goals to a group representing such a diverse range of languages, cultures and personalities is quite a task. **2-1-4-3** has made it feasible and brought both a discipline and a focus to the business which he embodied.

Many quotes have been attributed to Dr Lyons but the one that resonates most with me, with Aidan, and I think many of the people he touched was, "Why should my dreams for you be greater than your dreams for yourself?"

Dr Mark Lyons, President of Alltech.

Dr Mark Lyons, President of Alltech with his father, the late **Dr Pearse Lyons**, Founder of Alltech, Inc.

Effective v. Ineffective goals

Goal setting is a critical part of the planning process. The business literature talks a lot about "stretch" goals: goals that are substantially bigger and more difficult to accomplish. Stretch goals typically involve creative thinking and ambition on the part of the person or team trying to achieve them.

Setting ambitious goals must be done with care. Poorly chosen goals, especially those imposed from above, your boss or your boss's boss, can lead to problems with teams and individuals who are overwhelmed by a too-challenging goal, uncertain of where to begin, and afraid of negative consequences for failing to meet unrealistic expectations. High levels of stress may result in absenteeism, unnecessary risk taking, unethical behavior, and/or increased staff turnover. Goals should be challenging yet achievable, and managers need to be prepared to review and adjust goals as required.

The involvement of the team in the **2-1-4-3** process helps reduce the chances of unrealistic goals, and to minimize negative staff reactions to changes in firm strategy. Rather than imposing goals through a top-down process, they emerge through team involvement. The **2-1-4-3** process also allows for continuing flexibility in strategy design.

Stretching goals

Goal setting has always been a critical part business planning. Business books frequently talk about "stretch" goals: that is goals that are substantially bigger and more difficult to accomplish than those people usually set for themselves.

Stretch goals must be done with care. Managers sometimes make the mistake of setting goals that are too big that instead of encouraging a higher level of achievement serve to demoralize and demotivate teams who feel achievement to be beyond their capabilities.

This leads to the wrong behaviors, misleading or dishonest reporting, setting ultra-low targets in subsequent sales periods, disengagement, or undermining of the leader's goals in internal and external (customer) situations. Unrealistic stretch goals heighten stress levels and can result in absenteeism, unnecessary risk taking, unethical behavior, and/or increased staff turnover.

Numerous examples of the failure of stretch goals abound, from the implosion of the Soviet Union under the weight of 5-year plans, to the explosion of the Space Shuttle as managers ignored key information about the failure of the o-rings valves.

Goals should be challenging yet achievable, and managers need to be prepared to review and adjust goals as required. **2-1-4-3** overcomes this through the involvement of the team in the process, and this helps reduce the chances of unrealistic goals being set minimizes negative staff reactions to changes in firm strategy. Rather than imposing goals through a top-down process, targets emerge through team involvement. The **2-1-4-3** process also allows for continuing flexibility in strategy design and can result in top to bottom belief in the process and the ability to achieve superior results.

"I have used **2-1-4-3** for over 20 years in my career and find if to be a powerful tool in aligning sales and marketing goals, clearly a critical challenge in this era of digital disruption."

Catherine Keogh, Kerry Foods, VP Strategic Marketing and Business Planning

"The **2-1-4-3** method is not merely a switch in the "order" of planning. With the shift in order, there are new questions and thought processes that arise. The new questions and thoughts will drive disruptive change, not linear growth/change. This change, with the method's recommendation for including many levels of the organization, drives ownership of the plan to the entire organization. It makes one think about change, energy and focus. The focus should not be on fighting the old ways/thought processes, but on how we build the new methods."

Don Marquess, Owner, DM Group Consulting

"Everyone talks about the importance of stretch goals. **2-1-4-3** actually produces them."

Tom Koch, Director of Organizational Development, Ridley, Inc

"Simple advice summed up in this one line, 'Stretch goals are meant to push the team or individual into uncharted territory.'"

Camillus O'Brien, Managing Director, FMII Graduate

Your 2-1-4-3 process

This book is designed to help you work through the **2-1-4-3** process. Each stage of the process is spelled out and aligns with the enclosed color chart in the back of this book.

Structure

There are many ways to write up the **2-1-4-3** chart but for teams the most productive and efficient approach is to organize the process into three phases. This approach does best with a moderator, ideally somebody with a good understanding of the operation or organization, but not too closely aligned with any one person, group or agenda.

In the first phase, the team members carry out each of the four stages individually, and have the moderator collate the results. To maximize frankness and creativity, the team members should be encouraged to work individually, with the assurance that the moderator will anonymize the results (hence the importance of a moderator who is seen by the team as an honest broker). It is important that even points perceived to be outliers are included in the summary.

For the second phase, the team meets. Depending on the team, the moderator or designated team members can present the consolidated findings from stages 2 and 1 in a discussion format. Strong themes that emerge, and corrections or enhancements of the information collected for each stage should be noted and the findings written down. The **2-1-4-3** chart enclosed at the back of this book is available in a variety of formats, so that it can be used during this part of process.

After a break (where any changes or updates needed for stages 2 and 1 are made), the consolidated findings from stage 4 are presented. This is where all the elements come together and where a moderator or designated facilitator can be particularly helpful. The discussion should be free-ranging enough to allow new and creative approaches to come forward yet grounded in the understanding of where the organization is in its priorities, objectives and resources.

The diagram on the opposite page represents various companies that have come about as a result of a disruptive vision or idea. In some cases, the company was a start-up and created its own industry, in other examples, a well-established start-up segued (and disrupted) a current industry.

Present:
Where we are (really!)

The stages of 2-1-4-3
2. Present: Where we are (really!)

The **2-1-4-3** process starts with the here and now: Where are we right now? The key to this stage is HONESTY. What are the key characteristics of the organization? The approach is fact seeking, emphasizing neither the positive nor the negative.

Starting with the present, instead of the past, is more than a cosmetic change. Starting in the present disrupts your usual thinking pattern, which creates opportunities for fresh thinking on familiar topics. Now has immediacy to it that the past simply does not.

Understanding where you are in your competitive environment is the crucial first step. The usual analytics (P&L statements, market share analysis, customer analytics, SWOT analysis, etc.) should be used judiciously. Team members should know the headline numbers for their areas of responsibility, and those numbers should inform their input, but the focus here is on understanding the implications of the numbers, what is happening in the competitive environment and what business the company is actually in. Relying on analytical tools too much at this stage can be a distraction.

Analytics offer a quantitative picture, but a qualitative overview is also necessary.

By changing the focus and starting with identifying what you want to know first, you are better able to choose which type of tools is the most appropriate.

What is the business (customers) that we have?

To answer this, you will need to establish several criteria. Start by determining the direction your industry is headed as well as your position within the industry.

What direction is your industry headed?   Growing   Stable   Shrinking

Then note the percentage of the industry that is yours. This will determine whether there is room for growth in your current industry.

What is your industry position?   Leader   Follower   Niche

Sometimes this results in a debate about how you define your business, but that is good also!

What is your market share?   %

Another important consideration is the outside factors that affect your business. This is a fairly open-ended question and can include factors such as economic, regulatory, technological, etc.

List outside factors that affect your business:

Consider what type of resources you have available. This can be both assets you are currently using (e.g., advanced technology) or something that is underutilized (e.g., a strong marketing department). Just make sure you list as many as you possibly can. It will be important later when you are trying to tackle your goal.

Make a list of barriers in your industry as well.

If you are working with a group, it is useful to ask the participants to answer these questions separately and pool their responses. Be sure that the group understands that blunt honesty is essential. The quality of the final plan will reflect the soundness of the information it is built upon. Also, be prepared for unexpected, even surprising answers. Your team's understanding of your competitive environment may differ substantially from yours. Whether you agree with their views or not, treat their views as a useful learning tool and be prepared to question your own assumptions.

"One of the major reasons that results in a dysfunctional organization is poor interpersonal communications. Research from Harvard Business School suggests it is as high as 87%.

My own background in working with organizations in the field of emotional intelligence involves using the **2-1-4-3** model to help teams achieve clarity and focus on where the business currently is, help them articulate clear goals and objectives where they want to be in the future and to appreciate the key strengths and value each individual contributes to the team.

I find the **2-1-4-3** model invaluable in achieving consensus around a shared vision."

Deirdre Murray,
Managing Director,
People Resources

Case Study - Ireland

Visualizing a brave new step to create a billion dollar start-up

How does a start-up agtech company introduce game-changing technologies to an industry that is reluctant to embrace innovations, follows steadfastly to tradition and where the graveyard of tech disappointment is full of recent failures?

In 2011, brothers David and Ross Hunt found themselves as part of a four-director team to Comex, a grain trading company that dealt in futures trading. Upon an initial **2-1-4-3** analysis of the company, David and Ross realized some parts of its futures trading and decided to upend the business platform. The company grew 40% each year for the next two years.

Doing another **2-1-4-3**, the brothers realized there was potential to grow and build the business in an altogether new direction. In stage 2, assessing where the company was, they realized that it had new resources and strengths that were not being used: David and Ross' software experience. They also knew that the agriculture industry had no proper means of capturing data. The industry was stuck using archaic methods, hindered by poor technology utilization and dated software programs. Immediately recognizing this key breakthrough opportunity, the brothers approached the board for support for a new venture. Unfortunately, the board was so pleased with the growth achieved over the last two years that it decided against venturing into a new risky platform.

But the understanding of the resources they had and the industry trajectory that they had gleaned from assessing where they were led to an intuitive realization: If they could develop a low-risk, low-cost way to collect useful data they could bring real changes to the industry. As David explained, "If you can't measure something, you can't improve it."

cainthus

Over the next months, they recruited Dr Robin Johnston who had extensive experience with vision and artificial intelligence applications. He would bring about the means of collecting the information while David and Ross would manage the data, find solutions, and present them to customers to achieve cost savings. And so Cainthus was born.

Cainthus represented a rare meeting place of the agriculture and technology worlds. It blended knowledge of agriculture, science, software and business, to create a unique differentiating factor. For the first time, the agriculture industry could use data driven solutions to reduce inefficiencies in food production and facilitate more effective, environmentally sustainable use of land. The machine vision software that Cainthus developed enabled them to turn visual information into actionable knowledge.

The **2-1-4-3** process opened up new possibilities and, instead of resting on their laurels, they realized an even more exciting opportunity awaited them.

Past:
How we got here

1. **Past:** How we got here

In the **2-1-4-3** process, the past is considered through a specific lens to keep to identify the elements that are still relevant to the future. In many organizations there is a focus on past achievements in the business plan, often built on continually updating a set of analytic data. The **2-1-4-3** process takes a disruptive approach, and challenges participants to think differently by asking the question: How did we get here, and does it still matter?

To begin here, determine your fundamental core business. Most particularly, have you always had this business? If not, how have you diverged?

Questions challenge you to identify aspects of the business that have changed and are now irrelevant or outdated ways of thinking or doing business.

What are some highlights or historical milestones achieved thus far?

Finally, determine your company's historic strengths and weaknesses.
List all of them, and then decide which are still relevant.

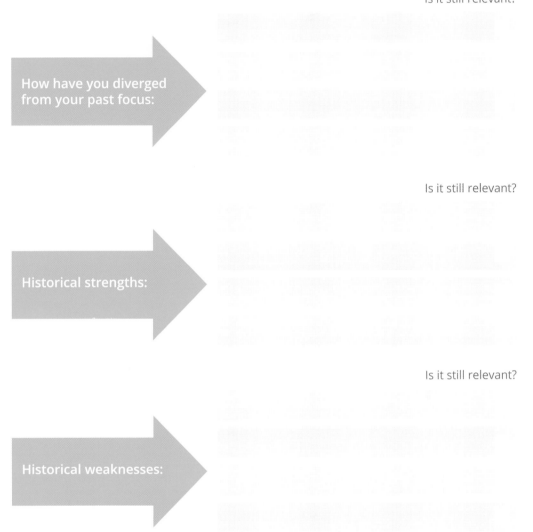

Is it still relevant?

How have you diverged
from your past focus:

Is it still relevant?

Historical strengths:

Is it still relevant?

Historical weaknesses:

The key to this stage of the **2-1-4-3** process is to keep it brief and factual. When reviewing the past, it is important not to focus on the negative, and in particular to avoid excuses as to why things are the way they are, assign blame or provide explanations as to why things can't be changed. This may seem counterintuitive, because the traditional view is that recognizing past mistakes is an essential part of doing better in the future, but the key in the **2-1-4-3** process is to identify old assumptions that can challenged or discarded. Knowledge, insight and inspiration can result, which in turn can lead to new ideas in stage 4.

Case Study - United States of America

Remaking a media company in a digital age

WATT Global Media celebrated 100 years in business by using **2-1-4-3** to chart the way forward.

These are challenging times in the media world. Although WATT is seen as an innovator in their target segments where they are active, providing exceptional business content and solutions to agricultural production and companion animals, they are facing the same issues as other media companies.

2-1-4-3 provided a roadmap for the development of WATT's Market Leaders initiative. As a provider of business information to specific industry segments their business model is based on bringing buyers and sellers together, professionals across the globe who are involved in the business of these industries, decision makers and influencers at the leading companies. These buyers are the high-value targets that sellers (those in genetics, animal health, animal nutrition, equipment and supply solutions) seek to reach with their information. The WATT sales team leverages deeper reach capabilities to these high-value targets by showing the ability to deliver the sellers' messages to these hard to reach professionals through specialized targeting and aggregation. The **2-1-4-3** process made it clear to the group that they needed a different approach that went beyond acquiring names through the typical list rental basis, but rather an approach that involved multiple departments across the organization and a higher value end result.

The Audience Development department performed a comprehensive audience evaluation to find out how many people in their database represented the leading companies in each industry and categorized these individuals as Market Leaders (stage 2).

The behavior of the Market Leaders was compared to the rest of the audience. To review "How we got here," (stage 1), they gathered representatives from the Audience Development, Content, Marketing, Sales and Technology departments to exchange information about how each could contribute to the initiative. These meetings ultimately forged a common understanding of the roles required to attract, engage, and retain audiences in the Market Leader segment.

Ambitious goals were set (stage 4) to increase the penetration with market leaders and set ways to measure and track these goals. This identified the need for additional tools and the creation of a requirements document so that the technology department realized the need to source a new platform to provide new level of capabilities to delivering messages to readers when they are engaged in specific behaviors on its web sites.

Together, the acquisition of acquiring the new technology and implementing the tactics on the Market Leader initiatives and measurement, led to breakthrough results.

Future:
Where we
want to go

4. Future:
Where we want to go

Having built an understanding of the present, and reviewed the past for relevance, the team can look to the future in the broadest sense. If your team has been working individually, this is where they should come together.

It is helpful to have answers from the questions in stages 2 and 1 synthesized and ready and use that information to lay the groundwork for the next set of questions. What is the topline goal of the organization? What opportunities are there? This could be industry trends, areas of customer growth potential or products you might be underutilizing.

What key breakthrough opportunities does this identify?

What are the resources required to achieve this goal?

Now, what types of barriers do you face when trying to achieve the above breakthroughs? How will you differentiate? How will your suppliers be affected? Are there political or regulatory challenges?

Paradoxically, the bigger the goal, the less complex it is compared to smaller, more incremental goals. For example, the number of steps required for a salesperson to increase sales 10% is at least as long as the number of steps required to double or triple sales and might even be longer. Generally, the more complex the initiative, the more incentive there is to narrow the steps to the fewest that will get you to the goal. In turn, you can focus more energy and resources on fewer action points.

A range of goals will emerge from the discussion of the questions in stage 4, so prioritizing, consolidating and selecting is essential. The objective is to identify the big vision, then break it down into more specific goals or targets. These goals should be ambitious but SMART (i.e., specific, measurable, attainable, realistic and timed).

These goals are an important part of accountability, but they are also an important step in moving from the big picture to the next step in the process: making it happen. The facilitator should leave considerable latitude to ensure that a range of ideas and views are on the table.

Mixing creative thought with critical thought can often smother one another, and so, the time should first focus on the creative side and then the critical side, preferably with a lengthy break in between. For example, completing creative thought in an afternoon session and then working on the critical thought the next morning is ideal. If time does not allow, then at minimum a good stretch break in between should occur.

Key breakthrough opportunities for growth:

1

Market Goal

Barriers

Resources Required

2

Market Goal

Barriers

Resources Required

3

Market Goal

Barriers

Resources Required

Case Study - Ireland

How to bake the right decision

Spanning three centuries, Bretzel is the oldest bakery in Dublin. The current owner, William Despard is an engineer by training and a true believer in what 'real' bread can and should be.

Over the last number of years, he has built a small but very strong management team and has brought Bretzel through a series of improvements and challenges, including expanding the premises, getting quality certifications, and putting in systems and processes that allow the company to make handmade, artisanal bread consistently, reliably and efficiently. As a result, turnover doubled, and operational issues are minimal. For the first time in many years, Despard was able to take a real vacation, and came back buzzing with ideas for growth and expansion. Some of these ideas were mutually contradictory and there were simply too many to pursue simultaneously. When he asked me for ideas I suggested he and his team run a **2-1-4-3**.

A day was set aside for an out of office strategy session. In advance of the meeting the four senior managers each completed answers for the stages of the **2-1-4-3**, submitting them to a moderator. In this case the moderator was a director of the company who is actively involved but does not have day-to-day responsibilities and so it struck a balance between familiarity of the person, but not someone who is operationally present. While participants varied in the time they took to answer the questions it was not difficult for any of them.

Collecting the responses, the moderator integrated them and prepared summaries of each. For the first session, summaries of stages 2 and 1 were presented prompting a useful debate about types of bakeries and types of customers, and what competitive space the company occupied. After a short break, which included integrating and updating the material from the first session, findings from stages 4 and 3 were reviewed. By late morning an entirely new strategic option had emerged from the conversation, which was sketched out and added to the long list of options already submitted.

After a lunch break, an outside business consultant arrived, and the management team presented the cumulative findings of the **2-1-4-3** stages. In answering a question from the mentor as to how the competitive space that Bretzel was in could be protected, it became clear that the entirely new strategic option was the only one that would protect that space, offer a path to strong growth, but would stay true to the firm's core competences and values. The rest of the day was spent sketching out stage 3: How we will get there. The net result of the day was a clear, focused strategy, with a 12-18-month implementation framework, with clear goals and roles for an excited and motivated team.

Bretzel has now run the **2-1-4-3** three times in five years and seen its turnover increase three-fold in those years. Not a bad return for a traditional business.

The big rocks of life - putting focus & time into the critical things

Consider the 'big rocks of life' theory as an analogy for stage 4. Once the main opportunities have been identified, next is putting them in the desired order of achievement.

A teacher filled a jar with rocks and asked her students, "Is the jar full?" The students replied, "Yes, of course."

The teacher then took pebbles and filled the jar again, shaking it down between the rocks. She asked her class again, "Is the jar full now?" This time, the students were not as certain.

The teacher then brought out a bucket of sand and proceeded to add still more to the jar. "What about now?" she asked. By now they were on to her and unanimously replied, "No!"

She smiled, reached below her desk, and pulled out a pitcher of water and filled the jar to the brim. "What is the lesson here?" she asked. One student suggested that no matter how full you think something is, you can always fill more in it. But the teacher shook her head and replied, "But what if I had put the water in first?"

"The big rocks represent your goals and what's most important to you in life. You must put them first or you will not achieve them."

Road ahead:
How we will
get there

3. Road ahead:
How we will get there

This final stage is crucial, because it is the translation of ideas into action, and carefully crafting the details are central to the success of the project.

In stage 3 you create the roadmap by which you and your team will work to make goals become reality. It should be a fun experience, because the process of creating the goal has been a team journey, and there should be enthusiasm and buy-in from all. Stage 3 evolves organically from the analysis and goal setting stages of the process. A critical component of the process is to create an environment which is positive and collaborative, where the collective imagination and knowledge of the team present come into play.

For the outcome of this stage to be successful, it is most crucial that the details are specific and clearly communicated. The chosen target goals must be identified with the expectations outlined. Those responsible for ensuring the success of each component of the goal, each action, must also be clearly identified and the expected results outlined as well as the pre-determined timeline showing when the task or action is to be completed. Stage 3 makes it possible to fill this out in a way that all feel ownership and comfortable with the outcomes.

Goal

1

Action

Department / Person   Follow Up Date

2

Goal

Action

Department / Person   Follow Up Date

3

Goal

Action

Department / Person   Follow Up Date

Case Study - Ireland

So now you are ready to brainstorm, what next?

After no growth in more than four years, an under-performing team gathers for a strategy retreat.".

I invited the team to Glendalough, a valley well outside of the distractions of Dublin and formerly the site of an ancient monastery, where the hermit monk Kevin had gone to meditate and pray, an ideal location for a retreat to elicit fresh ideas.

Once we got past the usual negativity including excuses and complaints as to why flat sales were a consequence of the market prices, poor customer perceptions of us, mistakes by previous managers or favourable relationships with our competitors, I asked each manager to list their most difficult challenges/accounts and the primary details of large ones where we had no business. This was stage 4 in the **2-1-4-3.** Each of the attendees identified 2-3 targets and then all 30 attendees were invited to contribute questions and suggestions about how to make breakthroughs in the form of an open forum, a negative-free space.

Fascinatingly as the exercise evolved I found myself contributing less and less: The power of the group discussion took over. It transpired that many in the room had valuable knowledge about their colleagues' targets, even those not in their country, including formal, business data, information about decision making processes, details of outside influencers, but also informal ways to get meetings or generate leads, and background on the interests/family/ education of key decision makers. By the end we had a long list of follow-up actions for each target and clear program of what the sales manager needed to do next. This was stage 3 of the **2-1-4-3.**

Over the next six years, almost 80% those key accounts identified in the retreat began doing business with us, and more importantly the momentum and positivity of cracking these accounts was part of an overall regional sales increase of 400% or a compounded 28.5% per annum. So **2-1-4-3** worked in a spectacular way, and provided the roadmap for the company as to how to achieve transformative sales growth.

Aidan Connolly

Case Study - United States of America

2-1-4-3 in practice

No better evidence of the power of the **2-1-4-3** in practice exists than the Alltech story. This private company grew from start-up capital of $10,000 to a turnover of over $2 billion in just over 35 short years.

In an historically conservative business-to-business environment this was no mean feat - particularly given that many of the company's most successful products were waiting to be invented. One of the keys to continuing that success was the frequent use of the **2-1-4-3** process.

Visionary leaders, especially entrepreneurs, typically focus on the desired future results, and try to figure out a way to get there. They start with the goal and focus quickly on actionable steps that will make their end goal or dream a reality. In real life, however, the number of truly visionary leaders is small, and more importantly banking on extraordinary or serendipitous insights is a high-risk approach to business planning. Adjusting traditional **1-2-3-4** approaches into the **2-1-4-3** process creates a framework for constructive disruptive thinking.

Alltech is a top-5 animal health company, focused primarily on natural nutritional supplements for animals. From its founding in 1980, it has set ambitious stretch goals. Its founder, Dr Pearse Lyons, started the business with just $10,000 in capital, and in the jargon of the day set a series of "big hairy audacious goals" (BHAGs) including $100 million by 2000, $500 million by 2005, $1 billion by 2012 (described in a 2008 Harvard Business School case study) and then $4 billion. The animal nutrition sector continues to grow, but not quickly enough to meet these aggressive timelines!

Throughout the process, Alltech gained a deeper understanding of turning stretch goals into action-oriented plans, for which it applied the **2-1-4-3** model. In 1999 sales were less than $100 million and the goal of reaching $500 million in sales was announced. Starting the Alltech team evaluated where the company was (stage 2) and found that sales were divided across several hundred products, with commensurate challenges in both sales and production. The company arrived at this position through an entrepreneurial spirit which had percolated through the company (stage 1), with continuous launches in both new products and new markets. A top line target of $500 million (stage 4) could be broken down into product categories. It became clear that focusing on just six core product areas (known as the Big 6) should be the key to the strategy (stage 3), remaining within existing core competencies that could be backed by patents, strong branding, deeper focused research and production expertise giving technological and cost leadership. The "Big 6" strategy involved both top-down aspects as well as bottom-up, particularly by removing ancillary costs of the previous lack of focus, improving quality and reducing "noise" in marketing communications.

Dr Lyons later announced the goal of making Alltech a $4 billion company. As the leadership team reviewed where the company was (stage 1) and how it got there (stage 2), it was immediately clear that achieving bigger goals changed the road ahead (stage 3). An organic growth path was no longer sufficient, and acquisitions would be necessary. A range of options, including expanding into traditional animal health products, pharmaceutical or vaccines, moving into the human health field and expanding the company's footprint in crop science were all considered, but rejected. These alternatives would not have the transformative effect of growing and securing the core business within the organization's key competencies. So Alltech's big decision was to choose to focus on acquiring organizations with strategic competencies it didn't have, specifically those working directly with farmers, either producing specialized premixes or other services on-farm. Over the course of five years (from 2011 to 2016) Alltech acquired 14 companies in nine countries.

As Alltech closes in on the $4 billion target a new target of $10 billion is expected. Again, the **2-1-4-3** process is being used to re-assess where the company is, how it got here and how it is going to get to the $10 billion target. The **2-1-4-3** process allows the leadership team to quickly and meaningfully review and re-evaluate the strategy. This time the acquisition focus has changed, with Alltech positioning itself to compete on many levels within the food and feed industries, while increasing its presence geographically. This alignment between ambitious targets and strategy through the **2-1-4-3** process has been instrumental, allowing Alltech to achieve goals that might otherwise seem unrealistic or unattainable.

Putting it all together

The **2-1-4-3** process was designed to encourage disruptive thinking in a constructive process. It can be used in a wide range of situations, including sales, marketing, technology or even personal planning.

Individuals can prepare their own **2-1-4-3** to achieve their individual goals within the **2-1-4-3** of the larger team, or for their own life objectives. In meetings the focus should be on stages 4 and 3, as this is where accountability and action happen.

The plans that come from the **2-1-4-3** process are a living document. At the end of the **2-1-4-3** process it should be possible to create a one-page document that makes the goal clearly visible at a glance, while capturing the necessary level of detail in terms of actions and accountability.

An example of this visual is found at the back of this book. It can be used as a template for printing the plan in an 11x18 or A3 format.

Wonka Industries— prototype of a 2-1-4-3

Confidentiality limits the amount of detail that can be shared by an individual company's **2-1-4-3** process, so we have aggregated a prototype to demonstrate the **2-1-4-3** in action.

It is meant to represent the various **2-1-4-3s** I have seen throughout my years but is not meant to represent any one company in particular.

Wonka Industries, a fictional manufacturer of chocolate, has successfully built a loyal following of raving fans, and has considerable market share in their home market. They have built an iconic marketing program which has run on TV and radio over many years, creating tremendous brand loyalty. Much of its marketing has focused on Wonka's founder, a mercurial entrepreneur who was also a masterful promoter of the brand, but who had passed away ten years ago.

More recently, Wonka seemed to have lost its way and was no longer growing. Online critics have used Wonka's traditional feelgood packaging and appeal against it by portraying it as old fashioned and out of touch, specifically questioning the transparency of its supply chain, and particularly in sourcing its cacao using fair trade and fair pricing techniques.

Following the **2-1-4-3** process the Wonka management group identified multiple challenges; it was struggling to connect with younger consumers and had a very limited presence in social media. They had also made limited progress with some key targets, most of whom could be very large accounts, and any new business they had brought in was being offset by losses of other business. They felt they "were losing as much business out the back door as was arriving through the front."

Targets identified through the brainstorming stage were the following big actions:

1.   A new world-beating, best in class Facebook page needed to be created, which would require special efforts and expertise. This could not be done in-house and would require hiring an outside agency to create and curate it.

2. A sales team dedicated to visiting key accounts—specifically an international airline, a nationwide coffee shop chain and linking up with a reality TV celebrity to create a special branded line.

3. A task force to examine why new customers weren't more loyal and why they were being lost.

As the three major actions were identified, they were broken down and people were given specific tasks, responsibilities, time lines and metrics. Each of the three goals had the potential to increase the sales by at least 30%, and offered the potential to energize the company at all levels.

To improve the social media presence, specific individuals were appointed to work with an outside agency to get the right feel for how to craft the right message on social media platforms such as Facebook, Instagram and Twitter.

For the second objective, a Key Account (KA) team was drawn from the sales team along with employees from other functions such as administration, production and marketing, to ensure a dedicated team to follow-up quickly. Jointly, this group targeted customers and created an action plan.

Finally, another multi-departmental effort focused on lost business. A Lost Customer Report (LCR) was generated monthly and appropriate actions identified to address where the company was failing and needed to take specific actions to "delight the customers."

As the 4-3 unfolded many interesting discussions evolved. Was it possible for Wonka to source from specific farms or plantations committed to pay fairly, to not use child labor, reduce pesticide, etc.? Could Wonka use blockchain or similar technology to provide higher transparency than competitors? Could they offer a product where customers felt they had done everything to "Do the right thing"?

Wonka's 2-1-4-3 provided a clear path for growth. Initially uncomfortable and challenging but ultimately, positively energizing, Wonka Industries created a set of goals the founder would have been proud of.

Let's make a plan

2

Start here

Present: Where we are (Really!)

This requires a factual evaluation of where things are today based on numbers, market studies and competitor analysis.

Outside factors

LARGE CORPORATE COMPETITION
WITH INTERNATIONAL PRESENCE

Industry direction

X Growing   Stable   Shrinking

Industry position

Leader   **X** Follower   Niche

Available resources

STRONG MARKETING TEAM WITH
UNDERSTANDING OF DATA ANALYTICS

General industry barriers

HARD TO CROSS GEOGRAPHICAL
BOUNDARIES; COUNTRIES / CULTURES
LIKE THEIR "NATIVE" SWEETS

Current core business

CANDY MANUFACTURING WITH
FOCUS ON CHOCOLATES

Market share

22% OF U.S.   %

1

Past: How we got here

Evaluating the past as precisely as possible, and its implications for today and future actions.

Historical core business

CHOCOLATE MANUFACTURER THAT
TRIED TO SEGUE INTO OTHER CANDIES,
BUT CHOCOLATE IS CORE

Historical strengths

STRONG LEADERSHIP; PRIVATE
COMPANY, THEREFORE NIMBLE;
LEAN MANUFACTURING PROCESSES

Highlights and historical milestones

COMPANY REACHED 50 YEARS;
DARK CHOCOLATE LINE HAS
RECEIVED SEVERAL AWARDS

Historical weaknesses

SOCIAL MEDIA PRESENCE;
CUSTOMER RETENTION

How you have diverged from your past strategy?

WE HAVE NEVER DIVERGED
AND NEED TO!

4

Market potential / goal

1 SOCIAL MEDIA PRES

Barriers

LACK OF UNDERST

Resources required

OUTSIDE AGENCY

Market potential / g

2 KEY ACCOUNT

Barriers

NO SINGLE PE

Resources requi

CROSS-FUNCT

Market potenti

3 CUSTOMER R

Barriers

NO FOCUS

Resources r

SUPPORT

How we
re

e past as precisely as
its implications for
ure actions.

engths

EADERSHIP; PRIVATE

THEREFORE NIMBLE;

UFACTURING PROCESSES

nesses

A PRESENCE;

ETENTION

Future: Where we want to go

Establish between 1 and 3 breakthrou
that will transform the organization.
Linear thinking is not allowed. The 3
disruptive goals should feel possible
but uncomfortable.

Market potential / goal

1 SOCIAL MEDIA PRESENCE

Barriers

LACK OF UNDERSTANDING; NO TEAM APPOINTED

Resources required

OUTSIDE AGENCY CONNECTION WITH INTERNAL SUPPORT TEAM

Market potential / goal

2 KEY ACCOUNT GROWTH

Barriers

NO SINGLE PERSON OR TEAM APPOINTED

Resources required

CROSS-FUNCTIONAL TEAM NEEDED TO SEEK OUT AND OBTAIN NEW CUSTOMERS

Market potential / goal

3 CUSTOMER RETENTION

Barriers

NO FOCUS HERE; NEEDS METRICS + CONNECTION TO MAINTAIN

Resources required

SUPPORT IN THE FORM OF PEOPLE; LCR TEAM

Road ahead: How we will get there

List concrete actions to achieve the key breakthroughs. Specific metrics, people responsible and time-lines are the key.

Goal

1 SOCIAL MEDIA PRESENCE

Action

CREATE TASK FORCE

FIND AGENCY TO HELP ORCHESTRATE + MONITOR

Department / person

MARKETING LED BY MARY LUBE

Follow up date

OCTOBER 24

Goal

2 KEY ACCOUNTS

Action

DEVELOP TASK TEAM + FIND CROSS-FUNCTIONAL MEMBERS TO CONTRIBUTE + COLLECT INFO ON KEY ACCOUNTS

Department / person

ERIN KIRBY

Follow up date

DECEMBER 27

Goal

CUSTOMER RETENTION

Action

DEVELOP TEAM + DETERMINE METRICS (LCR) TO FIND CAUSES OF LOST ACCOUNTS; COUNTERACT CAUSES

Department / person

NICHOLAS POTOCKI

Follow up date

DECEMBER 29

2-1-4-3 works: validation through 1,200 leaders

For this book we conducted a survey of 1,000 executives, VPs and C-Suite directors to understand their attitudes and behaviors during business planning.

The responses were startling. Less than 25% of respondents work on a business plan in a team meaning that 75% work on it either alone or with minimal buy-in from others.

Why do managers not produce plans with the help of their team? Do they fear conflict, questioning and disagreements will bog the process down? Wouldn't it be better for the entire group to know what the main goals are?

The estimated length of time it takes to write the plan was also very surprising: Over half of respondents think it takes two weeks or longer but once written only 36% feel it is relevant for three months or more. Clearly managers and executives are spending a disproportionate amount of their time working on business plans that aren't relevant for very long, especially given the time spent on them.

When asked how long a typical business plan is, over 72% reported that it is more than five pages and almost 37% said 10 or more pages! Even more astounding is what people are doing with their hard work: 36% of respondents didn't show it to anyone or only did if someone asked for it. One last number: roughly 10% of respondents said it would be something they would openly discuss in a meeting room for comments by their peers.

How can business plans be effective if this is the way they are created and used?

Ideally business plans should involve all that are affected. They should reflect the group's decision making through actionable goals and timelines that demonstrate accountability.

A separate survey of 200 people conducted with managers who have used the **2-1-4-3** provides a sharp contrast. Over 80% of respondents said a **2-1-4-3** could be achieved in under a week with another 72% saying they used a team approach to write the plan.

In contrast to the prior survey the **2-1-4-3** chart is designed to be displayed publicly in the office, on a wall, in the lunchroom and to be open to all. The **2-1-4-3** is a one-page document that defines the group or company's main goals, the actions necessary to achieve those goals, who is to achieve them and within what timeframe. Visibility maintains accountability and open display ensures this.

The success of the **2-1-4-3** process comes down to three key factors. First, it moves the focus away from the past. Instead, the time that is typically spent revisiting past events is used for considering future opportunities.

Second, it is user friendly. It is applicable to almost any situation within an organization and by participants at many levels throughout the organization. Because it is a straightforward process that can be completed comparatively quickly, it does not require tremendous inputs of staff time and resources.

Finally, the structure of the process allows for involvement of the team in ways that allow for their creativity, experience and expertise to be expressed, while bringing them along the journey together so that the final plan has their buy-in and support.

The **2-1-4-3** order focuses the discussion on future goals and establishes the actions necessary to achieve that goal. The process is designed to encourage participants to think in non-linear ways, disrupting old thinking patterns. This creates the potential to bring substantial business breakthroughs that are focused on the future, not the past, and on the practicalities of how we get from here to there, from the present to the future.

Survey Questions	RESPONSES	
	Traditional Business Plan	**2-1-4-3**
Number of responses	1013	194
Is it a team effort?	23%	72%
How long does it take to prepare it?	Less than one week 30.31%	Less than one week 82%
How long is it?	1 page 6.9%	1 page 100%
How long does it stay relevant?	1 page 6.9%	Up to 6 months 70%
Where do you keep it after it's written?	Posted in a meeting room 10.37%	On your desk / wall 77%

'Eureka!' How imagination works to find big solutions

When Archimedes jumped out of the bath naked and ran about shouting, 'Eureka!' as he suddenly solved one of mathematics great problems he was actually doing what humans have done for centuries before him and since.

So why do great imaginative leaps, problem solving, 'Aha!' moments occur when enjoying a bath or shower, walking in the woods or some other repetitive exercise such as weeding or moving the lawn? Why is it when we are most inactive that our brains seem to be the most productive, at least with regards to imagining new solutions?

Scientists explain this by brain synapses. Basically, the faster your brain is working the more productive you are, but the less creative also. Answering emails, phone calls, fighting fires, reacting to stimuli, all of these require fast brain decisions and leave no room for the mind to wander and problem solve.

Conversely a brain engaged in slow, repetitive tasks can daydream, connect random events or solve other problems. As the brain slows (demonstrated by the speed of electrical synapses) it starts to find new previously unimagined solutions.

Finding that insight, epiphany or Eureka! moment can be manufactured by you or your team. Take the time to gather, study and think about all of the facts. Then create the creative moment. For an individual that could be the 3 Ws of walking, weeding or washing (shower/bath) but for a team it could be some activity such as a hike or team bonding.

The short of it is this: Big breakthroughs come from slow brains.

Growing
your business

Case Study - Netherlands

Fishing for right answers:
The Coppens **2-1-4-3**

Alltech acquired Coppens International, a successful, privately owned Dutch speciality fish feed company that had been in business for 23 years. The facility had the ability to produce 50,000 tonnes and was close to reaching capacity.

A partnership with a local fish farm allowed for research capabilities to evaluate its feeds and gauge the quality of raw materials.

Coppens International evolved from being a manufacturer of pelleted fish feeds into extruded feeds with the acquisition of a German company in 2012. The company makes high quality aquatic feeds, across a number of aquatic species, in over 60 countries, but when acquired by Alltech it required a significant capital investment to take it to the next level.

Alltech set a goal to make Coppens International the cornerstone of its global aquaculture business. It not only invested in the company itself but transferred employees there to demonstrate as much of its technology and know-how to create a truly international aqua feed brand.

Investment in the three areas defined was key to the company's development. First, a third production line was added, increasing capacity to 80,000 tonnes. Secondly the research facility was deemed to be key to the company's future, so it was acquired and became Alltech Coppens Aqua Centre, one of the company's global Bioscience centers. Lastly the company infrastructure needed an overhaul including a new ERP system to improve efficiencies and control from order to invoice, including nutrition and manufacturing.

As the three goals have been achieved the need to rebrand the organization has become clear. Coppens became Alltech Coppens, recognizing its past but also placing the company squarely at the heart of Alltech's fish business strategy, creating a company that is primarily focused on growing fish sustainably in its commitment to the future of feeding the planet.

Case Study - Haiti

Making the difference, sustainably

Following a devastating earthquake in Haiti in 2010, Alltech launched Café Citadelle, a fair trade, shade-grown, hand-picked 100% Arabica coffee.

Building on existing trade and resources, it aimed to develop a sales and marketing channel for Haitian coffee and serve as a sustainable source of income for Haitian families. Profits from sales go directly into a 501(c)(3) nonprofit foundation, helping to fund two primary schools on the island, in the towns of Ouanaminthe and Dondon. Taking responsibility financially for the two schools including teacher salaries, maintenance, supplies and meals as well as completing renovations for safety and sanitation was the best way to help.

Inspired by his visit to the island immediately after the disaster, Alltech founder, Dr Pearse Lyons believed passionately that education and a lifelong love of learning are essential to sustainability. It was clear to Dr Lyons that buying a product that the island people already knew how to grow well could have an immediate impact.

He found the ideal partner in Cacgava, a coffee co-op with 900 members located in Dondon, a small village in the mountains of northern Haiti. The coffee's name was derived from Citadelle Laferrière, the largest fortress in the Americas, next to which Cacgava and its member farms are located. The coffee is naturally shade-grown and a high quality, mild, mountain-grown Arabica.

In 2012 Alltech's Café Citadelle Coffee needed another shot in the arm. Following a meeting where we ran a **2-1-4-3** with the team dedicated to the project, it became clear that in order to be sustainable in itself it needed a critical mass of business; Café Citadelle needed orders by the tons, not simply pounds or kilos. Dr Lyons looked at the **2-1-4-3** chart with the conclusion that big orders were required. "Well where do we buy our coffee?" he said the team. "We have over 100 offices in the world, serving coffee, running events and giving presents for Christmas & the New Year. Why isn't it Café Citadelle coffee?"

As simply as that the insight was worked on, and the business was turned around.

Case Study - Brazil

2-1-4-3 mergers & acquisitions style

Approximately 12 months ago, Alltech decided to acquire the shares of Guabi in Brazil. The company has a tremendous history of and expertise in making animal feed. In fact, in Brazil, the word "Guabi" is synonymous with animal nutrition, and as such, has a very powerful hold on the imagination of the Brazilian farmer and consumer.

With that in mind, Alltech's acquisition positioned it with one of the strongest brands in the business and certainly one with a lot of historic influence. It is also clear that this is an organization that is highly focused on value-added.

Three things came about as a result of the acquisition. The company was very focused on aquaculture and growing that business. However, one of the challenges was that the business was not particularly profitable, or not as profitable as people had previously imagined. Alltech immediately focused on leveraging the relationship they had with their aquaculture customers around the world, combining the presence of a strong brand in Brazil with Alltech's strong brand in other countries, including the Coppen's brand, an aquaculture feed company, in the Netherlands. This was something that it brought to the table to demonstrate how to grow the business from the perspective of the international piece of the field of aquaculture.

The second area that came to the table was that while Alltech had expended considerable resources in marketing and was considered a leader in that area, the format with which Guabi engaged in marketing was actually much more cost effective. Their focus on using "best in class" people from outside the organization not only brought a lot of real value, but also had the effect of demonstrating what could be learned from other consumer businesses. Therefore, the strategy is to work with people who have experiences from quite different backgrounds with leading global organizations. Their presence in Brazil introduced a variety of more efficient ways of getting information, brochures, and other communication done more effectively.

The third area was looking at the sales process. Guabi's sales process was focused on a quarterly bid basis, which allowed it to maintain market share. On the other hand, this bidding process made it difficult to grow. In contrast, Alltech's sales process was very focused on adding value and the goal at all times was to gain sales. The combination of the two made it clear that a value-added approach that Alltech brought offered some potential new learnings for the Guabi organization. That, combined with the other adjustments which were made, generated considerable increases in sales. In the first two years, the amount of technology added was doubled on the basis of tonnes of feed sold and the number of animals being fed.

The **2-1-4-3** process was viewed as particularly useful because it allowed Guabi to learn from the Alltech organization what was working. But, it also allowed Alltech to learn from Guabi as well. It is often the case that the acquired learns from the acquirer, but the ability to use the process for learning both ways was particularly valuable and was a testament to the usefulness of **2-1-4-3** to engage in a different level of conversation and one which was obviously beneficial to Alltech by increasing the overall value of the company that it acquired through the communication.

 **Case Study -** United Kingdom

The footprint for growth: 2-1-4-3 for E-CO$_2$

Climate change. Global warming. Carbon footprint. No longer buzzwords, these issues are of concern to every person on the planet.

Businesses are facing higher scrutiny and measuring carbon emissions has become increasingly important, especially for those involved in farming and food production. Consumer awareness has pressurized global retailers and processors to establish more proactive and responsible supply chains and not only understand their carbon footprint but monitor and improve their carbon emissions.

E-CO$_2$, a UK-based auditing company, helps suppliers to McDonalds, Arla Foods, Tesco and other food companies determine what the environmental effect is of the food they sell to consumers.

Previously family-owned, The E-CO$_2$ Project had successfully functioned in the UK as an environmental analysis specialist. It was acquired by Alltech, leading to a monumental change in emphasis for the business, coupled with a complete overhaul of mindset and culture. E-CO$_2$ was now part of a global business of which the goals, desires and aspirations were immediately on a different level than they had been previously.

Scaling a local business to international level presented numerous challenges in expanding its service offering. One of the biggest was that of communicating the realities of the sources and causes of farm carbon emissions on farm to various audiences and stakeholders, a challenge only made greater when taken to an international scale. E-CO$_2$ also found itself having to educate Alltech management in understanding where emissions come from, and that measuring and improving emissions holistically leads to improvements in efficiency, profitability and sustainability.

Alltech E-CO$_2$ has worked extensively to engage customers and inform them of the opportunities reduced environmental impact presents. General manager Ben Brau said, "There is a common misconception that sources of emissions such as fuel and electricity contribute the most significant amounts of carbon to the footprint of meat or milk.

The most significant emitters by far are the animals themselves and the production of their feed. For example, carbon footprint of the average dairy cow is comprised of approximately 40% methane produced in the rumen and a further 20% from feed production."

Far from being negative this provides a significant opportunity for producers and the food supply chain. Making the farm more efficient, increasing productivity and employing best farming practices, allows farmers to reduce emissions and increase profitability. Alltech E-CO$_2$ created a program working directly with farmers to measure and monitor their efficiency, profitability and sustainability, before creating detailed solutions for improvement.

The next major task involved identifying those markets most suitable and appropriate for these services. Through communication and education, E-CO$_2$ was able to focus international opportunities and priorities including resource allocation, market acceptance, political stability and customer appropriateness. Key markets identified included France, Germany, Canada, Australia and New Zealand.

To better define potential client partners further research was carried out. Large global retailers and processors are familiar with Corporate Social Responsibility (CSR) documents that define their social and sustainability objectives over a period of time. By reviewing this documentation published online, Alltech E-CO$_2$ understood each company's intentions, allowing for a more targeted approach.

Ultimately, utilizing the **2-1-4-3** approach, Alltech E-CO$_2$ was able to recognize its current market position, determine how it could successfully partner with multiple retailer customers, and design an approach which made it relevant for international issues such as global warming and carbon reduction. Harnessing its parent company's global presence, this approach was replicated throughout the predetermined international markets.

The use of the **2-1-4-3** model ultimately allowed E-CO$_2$ to take stock of what had made the business a national success with farmers, and then allow for the development of ambitious plans to grow and progress internationally through expansion into retail clientele.

Connecting
with your
customers

Case Study - India

Creating better customers

Alltech's office in India has a strong focus in three key species: chickens, cows and fish. Their natural nutritional supplements have between 2% and 28% market share, depending on the product and the species, but all agree there is room to grow.

Historically strengths included a strong brand synonymous with quality and service. The sales team had not only sales skills, but a strong technical foundation that enabled their understanding of the nutritional benefits and applications of their offerings. Furthermore, recent investments had been made in local production and research. Analysis showed an overreliance on one product, albeit a shining star, to carry the rest of line. Additionally, it has been suggested that some of the more recent innovations developed centrally aren't well adapted to the local needs.

During the opening of the Indian research center, which the top 20 accounts attended, the manager, Sayed Aman identified a massive opportunity for deeper customer engagement, specifically focusing on demonstrating the company's commitment to research and science.

The **2-1-4-3** process also demonstrated the need to focus on important accounts and key consultants. During discussions, it was clear that many good customers could relatively easily develop into larger accounts. Secondly, it was determined there was room for growth in untapped markets outside of the current species groups currently serviced and that a launch of a new range of products could also drive those segments forward.

Barriers to growth, such as the recent devaluation in the currency made imports more difficult but in its favor, the team had a low turnover rate and as a result, a team of very experienced and motivated senior sales people. It also had strong connections with local nutritionists and the ability to offer data analysis and metrics to customers.

Taking the plan into action, the team decided to expand on the success of the Customer Engagement Day and to expand that program, inviting both current and potential key customers. Even more impact was achieved when larger potential targets were invited to dedicate 2-3 days with the team, understanding the full range of possibilities, and to help Alltech shape its local strategy to meet them or their customers real needs, generating insightful conversation and focused interaction.

This Customer Engagement Day initiative allowed Alltech to grow its reach into new markets, expand its product line and grow its business with current customers by refocusing marketing resources and attention on a single platform of hosted events, further establishing itself as a leader in nutrition and performance.

Case Study - Ireland

Keeping a clear view of your goals: using 2-1-4-3 in the non-profit sector

LIKECHARITY is an award-winning Irish company helping charities fundraise more effectively via text messaging (SMS), television, phone and online.

Fundraising on behalf of charities is a challenging business - as donors are increasingly concerned about the effectiveness of their donations, donor acquisition costs and making a return on fundraising investments present an ever-present challenge for charities.

LIKECHARITY has employed novel technologies coupled with unique process management solutions that guarantee costs are very tightly managed. Their market-leading lifetime donor values consistently ensure direct investment returns and their approach has attracted Médecins Sans Frontières, ActionAid, World Vision, Sightsavers, Oxfam, Trocaire, Focus Ireland, Merchant's Quay, Irish Guide Dogs for the Blind, Threshold and many others to join their list of clients.

The company faced a crisis when its owner and relatively young founder, Tadgh O'Toole passed away after a short illness. Chief Operating Officer and co-founder John Kyne was given the not inconsiderable challenge of leading the company and after running a **2-1-4-3** as a workshop with Kate Phillips Connolly he assembled his team and mapped out their future.

John explains, "Embarking on the **2-1-4-3** model was a truly enlightening process for our team. With our business fast evolving, the **2-1-4-3** model showed us very quickly that we were rowing in different directions without knowing it. The process also highlighted our clear strengths as a business and has given us a lot to work from as we embark on our next chapter.

The speed and simplicity of this business planning model make it very practical and implementable which is ideal for our small and fast paced enterprise."

In working though the **2-1-4-3** process we realized we weren't as aligned as we believed; in fact it surprised me to see how clarity over goal setting was improved as the process evolved. Concretely this led to a solution to the challenge of expanding the business internationally by partnering with one of our top clients. **2-1-4-3** has helped like charity make the next leap"

2-1-4-3's power to crystalize business planning decisions is arguably even more important for non-profit organizations, where the luxury of making mistakes, particularly in terms of expenditure on new ideas and innovations, does not exist.

Case Study - Hungary

2-1-4-3 to create dialogue

A Hungarian consulting group has used **2-1-4-3** very effectively both inside its company and outside in relations with customers. This is how Gáti Levente, founder of G-Dialog Group Bt, helps his employees and customers to reach their goals.

He states, "In 20 years of working with **2-1-4-3**, I have had the opportunity to use it in a variety of settings and situations. It's been not only saved me from losing customers, it's also strengthened my relationships with them. Internally, it's done the same with employees." Here's how he did it.

"My company is in the food business, and I had a meeting at one of our regional headquarters. The conversation was focused around executing good coaching techniques and we talked a lot about motivating employees. We had made some changes and set new development goals; it was clear that one thing we couldn't do was to lose people from upper management until the new structure was up and running solidly. We asked really key employees what their ultimate goals were with the intent to help facilitate these goals.

"One of the managers said his dream since he was young was to own and manage an exclusive restaurant. He thinks that in the next five years he will be able to do this, but of course he would have to leave the company because he doesn't want to be dishonest by focusing on his private business at work.

"In order to keep this talent happy, the top management decided they would help him to reach his goal, provided he stay on for the next three years. Then they would help him not only with his education (paying for the school and giving him extra days off for the exams, etc.) but also to help find him a good location for his new business. This resulted in a very focused, happy and loyal manager who worked very hard while at the company, but when he did leave, left the company with a trained employee to take his place as well as amicable relations.

"Another example of how **2-1-4-3** worked for me was in relation to a customer of mine. We had a meeting in which I was to determine why he was dissatisfied with a product we had sold him. It was my intention to neutralize his feelings toward the product, but the first phone call was pretty rough as he was very unhappy.

"I followed up by meeting him in person where he showed me his farm and as we were talking I used the concepts of **2-1-4-3** as a guide to help direct the meeting and determine the root concerns and possible solutions. When I got to stage 1, we discovered numerous common ground and people we knew, which helped to build rapport with this man. Then I asked him about stage 4, specifically inquiring about his big goals he wanted to achieve. I was surprised to learn that organizing an overseas trip for 50 people in his organization was a very important goal of his. He had promised to do it and was having a very difficult time since the budget did not allow for all the pieces he needed to accomplish this.

"It just so happened I had my own experiences and connections in the country of choice and I was able to help him to achieve his goal within the budget allotted. As a return he not only gave the product another try, but also agreed to purchase another and to introduce me to several potential customers as well. It was a big win-win for each side and I credit my understanding of **2-1-4-3** with the results.

"Every person has a **2-1-4-3**. In order to motivate somebody, it is good to know where he is now, from where he is coming, what his goal is and how he wants to achieve it. The last part is probably the most important. There is a risk in asking such questions from somebody. If you go through the questioning process and you do nothing with it, but instead focus on your own goals or your company's goals (as opposed to those of the customer), you will end up with either a frustrated employee or customer or perhaps none at all. If you are to ask the question, you must follow through with the response, but that is true with any process. What **2-1-4-3** does is make the question or concern clear and then align those involved in execution together."

Case Study - Scotland

Using **2-1-4-3** to help your customers get customers

A telemarketing company in Scotland had a brilliant idea: Why not perform a **2-1-4-3** with potential customers?

After all, don't their customers want to achieve big goals and grow substantially as well? Isn't it the business of the supplier to help them to achieve these goals?

During a workshop with Kevin Tuck, this company run by five women, was convinced to call 13 potential customers whom had never been sold to before and engage in a discussion with them using the **2-1-4-3** process. Expectations of success was very low, based on previous experience, however rather than trying to talk them into doing business, they just asked them what they wanted to achieve and what their goals were.

At the end of the phone calls, seven of the 13 companies became customers.

Kevin asked them to find out why these customers were suddenly willing to do business with them, so they called several of them back. The customers replied that for the first time, they felt someone cared about their goals and would be a part of achieving those goals, instead of simply trying to sell them stuff.

As Kevin says, "If you don't understand your client's needs and aspirations how can you expect to provide them with the products or solutions they really want? Finding out what they really want is done through your questions, not by what you tell them, and actively listening to their answers is essential to this."

As the maxim states: Customers don't care how much you know until they know how much you care.

Focusing on your team

Case Study - Ireland

Keen for clarity: Using 2-1-4-3 to get consistent, coherent goals

The Keenan company was formed in 1979. Over a period of 30 years the company transformed the unglamorous business of mixing food with metal machines for cattle into a very sophisticated and highly technological process using the internet of things and connected devices.

Financially however the company lost its way. By 2016 it was in financial trouble and needed an investor to survive. Alltech was that investor.

Led by Alltech's former crop division director Robbie Walker, the new management team assembled quickly to discuss future directions and avail of the resources offered by being owned by an organization with offices in 131 countries. A **2-1-4-3** process was conducted both by Walker on his own, the core team of nine managers, and later with a larger group of 40 representing those based in Ireland and elsewhere. "It was interesting to me to note the breakdowns in communication. What I knew we needed to do was different from what my senior managers said when they were asked to identify the three transformative goals for the organization. This clarity, from top to bottom, was the key to our success," Walker explains.

Keenan is facing a far more challenging market, and to some degree its recent slowness in continuing to invest in product development and innovation is causing those challenges. That said the **2-1-4-3** process has made it clear where investment, attention and managerial focus should be. "We need new products, to innovate with digital technology, open new geographical markets and consider new business segments, but the **2-1-4-3** has made me more convinced than ever of the value of a clear, focused approach," Walker said.

He continued, "The **2-1-4-3** has been an invaluable tool to rally the team behind clear, concise and consistent actions. For me, the most important part of the **2-1-4-3** process is that it provides a quick reporting and feedback system. It helps me cut through the noise. Each member of my team has committed to a small number of actions and when we communicate, we know what we should be communicating on. Deviation from the agreed actions means we are losing direction. The **2-1-4-3** makes communication quick and on-point."

Case Study - China

Breaking down walls in China; using 2-1-4-3 on social media

Finding the way to improve communication in a society with 4,000 years of history isn't easy.

Having traveled over 50 times to China, I am frequently reminded of the cultural differences: the avoidance of conflict, the importance of guanxi (relationships) and not losing face are concepts unfamiliar to those from other parts of the world.

Against this backdrop, I have found using **2-1-4-3** has been the tool to give the results I was seeking. Offering a real analytical tool, it has provided focus and direction within the Alltech Headquarters in Beijing, assessing the current sales situation and identifying a plan of action for yearly, quarterly and even monthly meetings. It helps determine the business opportunities in the market and gives an accurate portrayal of current customer market and developments, while allowing us to be creative and imaginative in our methods for achieving goals.

The Chinese use the social media platform WeChat extensively so the Alltech China team placed the **2-1-4-3** template in a shared Alltech China public WeChat account so that the whole group could see the goals and plans.

2-1-4-3 was in particular at the forefront when Alltech acquired Keenans. The team was initially skeptical of the appropriate business model for machinery but used **2-1-4-3** to identify the business opportunities in China that could benefit from the Keenan machinery and launched the iTouch service at a Dairy Symposium. The combination attracted a lot of interest from a customer perspective and has greatly increased reach to the thousands of dairy farmers in the region.

Chinese customers have also learned from the model to determine their own analysis of their businesses and where they would like to take their own companies.

Alltech has offered sales training and management development programs to these clients and in their feedback, they have highlighted the benefit **2-1-4-3** has brought to their business. "**2-1-4-3** is certainly another resource to promote relationships with customers, especially focusing on their issues in sales function, but it has also allowed us to align our own services to theirs," said the China sales director. "It's an incredible tool to facilitate discussion both inside and outside a company."

Case Study - Ireland

Annual growth of 45-60% in a mature market

Satisfaction for the individual or the team can be generated through growth - personal performance, academic achievements, improvement. Some sales teams achieve this through meeting or exceeding goals and targets while many do not.

Why? Teams often believe that the goals are unattainable, the goals are imposed from outside the team or the team feels it doesn't have the resources to make it happen. Alltech Ireland set and successfully have achieved aggressive goals, doubling sales in a two-year period. What makes this growth remarkable is that the market was perceived as being a mature, slow growing, traditional market with little potential.

Manager Cathal McCormack considers that, "My sales force are extroverts, strong at people skills but poorer at goal setting following a strategy." Using **2-1-4-3**, he set about focusing the team on specific objectives. The Irish agricultural market, particularly for milk production, has been seeing tremendous disruption. Younger, more ambitious farmers are displacing older traditional ones. These are expanding herds, embracing new technologies and very much seeing the world market as an opportunity for grass fed cows, with a focus on sustainability and profitability.

With clear objectives (stage 4) and very specific actions (stage 3), the Ireland team gained new energy. In quarterly meetings, each sales manager now presents a progress on their **2-1-4-3** with these three main objectives and confirms their plan for the following quarter. The valuable time of the meeting becomes very focused on how each objective will be achieved, outlining an exact timeframe around what needs to be done to achieve it. This helps to put clear focus on what actions need to be accomplished in a simple and uncomplicated way.

"Over the years I have used various sales tools to help me and my team identify clear goals and to have the discipline to follow through on the goals. After much experimenting I have found that the **2-1-4-3** model is the without doubt the best and easiest to use in helping my team to achieve their goals and drive sales performance to the next level," says McCormack.

 **Case Study -** European Union

Fermenting the right solution: Using 2-1-4-3 to drive innovation

Alltech's discovery that adding yoghurt bacteria with sugar helped to preserve grass in the form of silage in Europe was momentous and this led to the development of a significant market.

After many years of strong growth however the silage market had matured. The dry powder form was originally favored by most customers, and many expected private label brands, but the market was changing. Alltech was meeting customer expectations with year-on-year growth of around 6%.

Matthew Smith, the new global manager felt there was much more room for improvement and conducted a **2-1-4-3** with the team, with the goal of doubling sales in a three-year period. The **2-1-4-3** made it clear that the company was missing out on the potential to appeal to customers who preferred alternative methods of silage inoculation application such as liquid, which when compared to granular, had some deficiencies.

The dry form had a short shelf life, high inventory costs, required considerable storage space, particularly when compared to concentrated water-soluble forms that were a fraction of the package size, and could be activated when required. Combined, these factors applied significant cost pressure to the dry product supply chain. In response to the **2-1-4-3** outcomes Alltech's R&D team created a highly concentrated product that was flexible in its application rates, but also had the unique feature of being capable of being used with other preservation technologies.

In addition to launching new products the **2-1-4-3** also showed that Alltech would need to restructure its distribution network, terminating some agreements, and service some customers directly. Making these changes ensured that the goal of doubling sales in a three-year period was more than achieved.

Accelerate Start-up Growth

Accelerate growth via start-ups

The Pearse Lyons Accelerator (PLA) was set up to help companies who are involved in developing technologies that support the food and agriculture sector. In two years, the PLA has received 300 applications from 38 countries.

The inaugural cohort selected ten companies, all late stage start-ups. As such, they had already raised substantial funds, on average over $3 million per company. In fact, most already had customers and were well on the way to a profitable future. They covered areas of agriculture and food production as diverse as digital technology (drones, sensors, big data analytics) to alternative proteins and magnetics.

Alltech worked with Dogpatch Labs, an Irish based start-up hub and part of the Google network. Dogpatch Labs had never worked on a late stage start-up accelerator before so there was something to be learned from all ends. Although the program included many elements such as raising capital, pitch coaching, mentorship, marketing and communications, it was the **2-1-4-3** process that was judged by the group to have the most impact on their business.

While working through each company's **2-1-4-3**, the focus was on defining the three actions most likely to help them accelerate to the next stage of growth. "Burn-rate," a company's expenditure versus income, is a continual pressure for start-ups, and reaching breakeven is key to survival. Most of the **2-1-4-3s** identified specific sales territories the companies should consider, target accounts that would make the difference and how to use Alltech's resources to achieve these goals.

As an outcome of this process, the accelerator companies received a combined $50 million in qualified sales leads. MagGrow, an advanced magnetic spraying system, generated millions in sales leads itself and gained access to six markets. AgriWebb, a farm data management software company generated millions in qualified sales leads across four new markets.

 agrilyst

 HARGOL DELIVERING PROTEIN

 AgriWebb

 alesca life

 eFishery

 Tevatronic AUTONOMOUS IRRIGATION

 Greengage Enlightened Farming

 Moocall connecting you to your animals

 MagGrow Magnetic Spraying Systems

 MicroGen Biotech

 SkySquirrel technologies

 eggXYt

 SmARTBOW WE KEEP ANIMALS HEALTHY

VENCE

ENTOCYCLE

Pearse Lyons ACCELERATOR

DISCOVERING INNOVATIONS OF TOMORROW, **TODAY**

Case Study - Australia

Growing your
webb of contacts

With five generations of family farming, the founders of AgriWebb's had deep farming roots. Yet we held a belief in a "Silicon Valley start-up mindset." We participated in the inaugural Pearse Lyons Accelerator program for 15 weeks leading into Alltech's annual ONE conference.

This program exposed us to the **2-1-4-3** method and set in motion a series of events charting a course that culminated in opening a new geography, acquiring complementary farm management software market incumbent and raising two funding rounds, making AgriWebb one of the best backed agtech companies on the globe.

AgriWebb's moment of self-reflection during the Pearse Lyons Accelerator reminded us that our core strength was the market-leading usability of the product with an extremely low churn rate of 0.5% and solid market penetration of managing over one thousand farms.

While product engineering was our strength, one of our core problems was sales growth and overall company scalability. Taking stock of our market position found us the fastest growing farm management software in the southern hemisphere with the best development team, but found an unscalable sales model, no concern for customer success and ad hoc business processes. Operationally, the company was not ready to scale and be a global market player. We needed sales and support to catch up to the superior software, a product of significant energy and resource investment.

The **2-1-4-3** process led us to determine who our key target customer was, how we were going to solve their problems in order to scale up sales and grow to a point in which we could impact the global marketplace. Once we determined our best potential segments, we spent months with our target customers, understanding their pain points and working to solve their problems. It took time to really focus on the core problem and refine the solution. (It is very easy to get distracted and chase the shiny lights!).

The next step was outlining how we were going to achieve this. As founders, we had a global ambition from day one. We wanted to have real, tangible impact in a real industry. While AgriWebb's growth in Australia was comfortable, we needed to engage at a global level. Actions and resources needed to match ambition and aspiration. We needed to raise external angel capital and find the best engineering talent possible.

1. The targets

Examine the landscape and uncover key markets: UK, US and Brazil. A strict segmentation analysis enabled objective decisions.

2. The resources

Talent, function and planning. We needed to increase the team, our war chest and our advisor knowledge pool. We needed skills in growth marketing to drive a digital sales funnel, and sales strategy to scale revenue, product management to build the right tools to solve the right problems, advisors to open doors and provide strategic insights. All this while ensuring our customer remains number one.

3. Execution

In order to tackle new markets, the company needed systems, process and governance in place to be scalable in Australia and in new global markets.

How did we do it?

At the ONE conference we went hunting.

Our advisors, Aidan Connolly and Steve Schramm, 8-time SF Founder & StartX Mentor, introduced us to and enabled conversations with the right people in the right places such as Brazil, the UK and the US. Relentless shoe leather networking unearthed inroads into markets that might have seemed impenetrable. We took our product and represented it to those who could make impacting decisions, tirelessly working at demonstrating and unlocking unprecedented value and making strong trusted relationships.

It is through this process that we now have the team and the capital to execute and establish ourselves in the leading markets necessary to grow. Since the ONE conference, we have raised two rounds of funding. The first from strategic farming family offices and the second from the Wheatsheaf group, which is one of the most respected global names in agricultural investment. We executed a deal for capital and IP to hold us in a strong position to positively impact the global protein supply chain.

Through the Pearse Lyons Accelerator and the **2-1-4-3** exercise, AgriWebb generated $10 million of new sales leads across four new markets!

Written by Justin Webb
Co-Founder & Chairman of AgriWebb

Case Study - Israel

Making a leap! What is your one strategy?

Hargol FoodTech is an Israeli alternative protein company that specializes in grasshopper protein powder. Here is co-founder Dror Tamir, telling his story.

"We joined the inaugural Pearse Lyons Accelerator and greatly appreciated the opportunity it afforded us, including the instruction in the **2-1-4-3** process. Had we not undergone this exercise, we might not be where we are today.

"For Hargol FoodTech participation in the Alltech accelerator led to two immediate results. Firstly, a clearer product and company strategy for the company thanks to meetings and discussions with the Alltech team sharing their experience and applying it to the newly developing insect protein industry. It was a 'once in a lifetime' chance to leave behind the day-to-day activities of the start-up and look at the wider picture, realize the great opportunities we have and redirect our ship towards a greater vision. Secondly, a series of wins in international innovation competitions (five since completing the program three months ago and counting) that helped us close a round of funding.

"The **2-1-4-3** process helped us realize what are the big rocks we need to focus on in order to catapult Hargol's activity. Instead of trying to work out our daily challenges we were able to identify the greater tasks ahead of us on our road to become world leaders building a new insect protein industry. Understanding what we need to accomplish in order to meet our vision we were able to make better business decisions overcoming daily challenges quicker and pushing Hargol forward. For example, we were able to double our production capacity within three weeks with the same budget by deciding to focus on the grasshoppers growing while other side tasks were done by subcontractors instead of our employees. This change can now easily lead to us to double our capacity every two months relatively easy."

Dror Tamir
Co-Founder & CEO, Hargol FoodTech

Case Study - United States of America

Using **2-1-4-3** to hot-house your growth

Agrilyst is using data to accelerate the greenhouse and vertical farming industries. Their software platform is designed to help greenhouse operators run their businesses more efficiently and more profitably.

Greenhouses are an incredibly important tool for our agricultural system. We have to increase the volume of food production to meet the demands of our growing global population and we have to do this with resource constraints. Controlling the growing environment helps growers achieve this goal.

There are twelve million greenhouse acres producing vegetables. Flowers and cannabis are produced indoors. Growers are de-risking a farms; major threat—the weather. Technology is also more widespread indoors in comparison to field agriculture. However, despite using sensors and controls for climate, water, and lighting, more growers still use spreadsheets and paper records for most work-related processes.

Allison Kopf, the founder and CEO of Agrilyst, worked in the industry and experienced the pain of managing operations without real-time data and insights. It was clear that data was the key to improving resource allocation, crop yields, quality, delivery to customers, and profitability. Agrilyst has raised over $3 million from leading investors. The company won TechCrunch Disrupt in San Francisco in 2015 and was selected in the first cohort of the Pearse Lyons Accelerator.

According to Allison, "One of the most useful things we worked on during the Pearse Lyons Accelerator was **2-1-4-3** planning. When we were kicking off the accelerator, we were trying to make the transition from mid-market customers to enterprise customers.

We faced a few challenges in the process:

1. How to determine the product was ready for enterprise customers.

2. How to set pricing for two customer sets.

3. How to service separate products and customer segments.

4. How to scale.

"**2-1-4-3** planning is an effective way to look at the status of your company and identify the challenges so you can break down roadblocks enabling you to scale.

"We were able to focus in on specific geographies and how to refocus internal engineering and sales resources to focus on larger customers. As a result, we grew revenue 10 fold since participating in the PLA and our software is available in 10 countries servicing more than 800 crops.

"Following the **2-1-4-3** process, we reallocated our resources, moving some of what we spent on technology and development into sales and marketing. We hired a VP of Customer Success and built our first sales team. In selecting new investors, we strategically chose some who had the ability to help us expand into the market in China (such as Horizons, Argonautic and Onlan). We expanded from servicing only vegetable producers to offering products for cannabis growers as well. We were also able to focus our engineering efforts on the products that helped our growers the most, like releasing our mobile application to help manage crops and employee workflow."

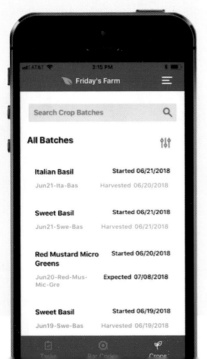

As Phil Chen, advisor at Horizons Lab said, the "computation cost is driven to zero and we now have the resources to monitor the growth, health and biology of every single seed. I see Allison and her team at Agrilyst as the interpreters of this data to secure future food sources."

Case Study - Ireland

Getting your start-up on TRAC

uTrac, a Dublin-based software company, started out as many tech start-ups do: meeting an internal need. An event management company involved with managing events for groups such as U2, The Rolling Stones, Madonna and other theater events and shows, needed a better system to manage complex temporary and zero contract labor teams.

All the off-the-shelf options were geared toward rostering relatively stable teams, so they built their own, spun it off into its own company and took their better mousetrap to the market. Over the next two years the founders struggled to make the company profitable. They had a solution for their own problems, and probably those of similar companies, but they wondered if the market was big enough to support it as a viable business. As one advisor noted, "There is a niche in the market, but is there a market in the niche?"

Joined by new shareholders when they started the **2-1-4-3** process, uTrac had faced down a multitude of challenges. Writing their own software, establishing it as a cloud based system, seeking and bringing in customers, marketing it through social media and attending leading tradeshows in Ireland and the UK had brought a certain amount of success, but the company had yet to make the leap from start-up to sustainable business. Growth was steady, but slow.

The small team of five used the **2-1-4-3** process to look at their existing success stories, especially with some larger 'Blue Chip' event organizers, and at the characteristics of those customers and realized that they had to refocus their strategy. Three key strategic elements were identified: (1) differentiate tiers of service that reflect the needs and potential of smaller and very large customers; 2) use automation to bring on board smaller customers with less direct staff time; (3) use artificial intelligence (AI) to meet the needs of very large companies, extending beyond the original industry sector. As uTrac's team began to address these three elements, two outside companies contacted the organization offering what seemed to be

instant solutions. One company was similar to uTrac, operating in complementary market segments, which would immediately bring in customers new industry sectors and new regions, and the other offered an AI system that was almost plug-in ready, and would allow uTrac to provide a strong, unique offering to very large customers in a number of new sectors.

uTrac's **2-1-4-3** proved to be helpful in evaluating these windfall opportunities. Stage 4 in the process helped uTrac see that these companies' competencies dovetailed neatly with uTrac's needs. Just as important, however, the process of working through the **2-1-4-3** (in particular, the '3' stage) helped uTrac to forensically evaluate these opportunities, see past the immediate attractions of these quick fixes, recognize the limitations of the potential relationships long-term, and discern what elements, and on what terms, would be of most benefit to uTrac. In the process, they realized that they could put in place a simpler AI solution internally that delivered comparable functionality without having to be dependent on an outside vendor for a key product feature. For a small, chronically over-worked team, **2-1-4-3** proved to be a simple, nimble way to get clarity of focus and both recognize and assess opportunities.

Personal
2-1-4-3

Personal 2-1-4-3

The **2-1-4-3** process can be as helpful in meeting personal goals (or private goals within the workplace) as it is to organizations. Just transition the points to help you identify:

2 Where you are today

- What are the main aspects of your life (work, social, family)?
- What stage are they in?
- What changes are coming?
- What outside factors affect your choices (financial, legal, abilities)?
- What resources do you have?

1 How does your past limit your future choices

- Is where you are where you are meant to be?
- How do your roots or past choices affect your future options?
- How do your past relationships affect your present relationships? Future relationships?
- What aspects of your present reflect parts of your past that are no longer relevant?

4 Identify your goals for the next year or next few years

- What is your big goal? Three big goals?
- What are the different ways to achieve that goal?
- What resources are required?
- How do each of those paths affect your current life?

3 Determine what action steps you need to reach your goal

- What resources do you have and / or need?
- What steps / tasks do you need to take?
- Who else do you need to carry out these steps?
- What is your timeline (including milestones)?

By definition, a stretch goal seems impossible at first, yet they are accomplished over and over again. You can use the **2-1-4-3** process to achieve any goal: learn a language, achieve career goals, and change your personal life.

As with the business version, your personal plan isn't developed and then abandoned: It is a living tool. Keeping it visibly in front of you and tracking your progress is an important part of the process.

Instead of being overwhelmed by the scale of your goals, or being waylaid by obstacles, the **2-1-4-3** process helps you lay out a plan in a set of achievable actions. If you use specific dates and times your **2-1-4-3** will be effective and ensure that your goal becomes reality.

2-1-4-3 final thoughts

The goal of creating high performing teams, enjoying success and celebrating reaching higher targets should be the desire of every manager.

From first coming across the **2-1-4-3** process over 20 years ago and perfecting its usage, this book and the process of writing it has taken far longer to finish than I, or others, imagined. Critically I wanted it to be a short book about a way of writing a short business plan.

2-1-4-3 has clearly demonstrated its value in transforming the business of large and small, for profit and non-profit, consultancy, consumer goods and business-to-business performance. It has produced 15, 25, 40 & 60% growth rates, even in markets that had shown no signs of that growth before.

So why not for you? In an age when transformation has never been more key, **2-1-4-3** is a planning model for the times we are in. Disruptive, yet focused.

Use it and tell me how it works for you.

Find me on Twitter:
@AJConnolly1

Find me on LinkedIn:
https://www.linkedin.com/in/aidanjconnolly

Acknowledgements

The origins of 2-1-4-3 are obscure. 2-1-4-3 came to Alltech through the late Kevin Davey who was based in Ireland and who readily encouraged and allowed us to take it globally. The first region to do so was Asia Pacific, which became the poster child as we quickly realized the power of 2-1-4-3 as a sales, marketing and business model.

Thanks to Kate for her support and joint authorship.

To Alexa Potocki, who contributed so much: writing, editing and delivering the final copy to our publishers.

I would also like to acknowledge many who made it possible, both those already credited and those who contributed to reading and making comments including Damien McLoughlin, Tom Koch, Declan Coyle. I like to thank Mary Lube, for all her countless hours of follow up, collecting contributions from all over the world.

And finally, to remember my mom Deirdre, who passed away recently, and who will always be remembered with love.

Who is Aidan Connolly?

Aidan Connolly is an unusual leader. Despite nearly 30 years of business experience, employed in one company, his role has changed so often his experiences mirrors that of senior executives or global consultants. He has worked with a full range of executive and managerial challenges, including direct experience of greenfield start-ups, high growth environments, turnaround issues, challenging economic environments and a wide range of political and economic systems.

He has leadership experience ranging from strategy to operations to production, as well as developing sales programs and cohesive teams that deliver strong results.

Connolly has worked in over 100 countries, lived in six of them and speaks five languages. He has worked in political associations, with state and national governments in the US, China, Europe and Brazil and international organizations such as the European Union and the United Nations.

Connolly has appeared as a commentator on radio and television, often being cited for his knowledge of the animal feed industry. He holds positions as adjunct professor of marketing at the Smurfit School of Business, University College Dublin and the China Agricultural University in Beijing.

He has published over 30 academic articles and is a regular contributor to social media where he is particularly active on LinkedIn and Twitter.

He is currently employed at Alltech, Inc. as the chief innovation officer and vice president of corporate accounts.

Please connect with him on:

LinkedIn **https://www.linkedin.com/in/aidanjconnolly**
or follow him on Twitter **@AJConnolly1**

Aidan Connolly
Chief Innovation Officer,
Vice-president, Corporate Accounts,
Alltech

Let's make a plan...